I'm Allergic to GREY HAIR

Author:
Nikki Gillis

Co-Author:
Doris Norwilla Brown Kimbrough

LAEL PUBLISHING

I'm Allergic to
GREY HAIR

Author:
Nikki Gillis
Co-Author:
Doris Norwilla Brown Kimbrough
Published by Lael Publishing, LLC
Winston Salem, North Carolina
www.LaelAgency.com

No part of this book may be used or reproduced in any form, stored in a retrieval system, or transmitted in any form by any means, electronic, photocopy, mechanical, recording or otherwise without written permission from the author. The only exception is for critical articles or reviews, in which brief excerpts may be used.

ISBN 978-1-7325344-2-1
Copyright © 2019 by Nikki Gillis
and Doris Norwilla Brown Kimbrough
All Rights Reserved
First Edition
Printed in the United States of America.

Table of Contents

Dedication

Preface

Chapter One: Salem Hill
page 13

Chapter Two: The Highest Birthday Party
page 23

Chapter Three: Colored Water
page 31

Chapter Four: God Accepts all Sinners
page 39

Chapter Five: Working for Free
page 51

Chapter Six: Stand for Something or Fall for Anything
page 63

Chapter Seven: Mother's Day for the Motherless
page 79

Chapter Eight: Get Off the Bus
page 87

Chapter Nine: Traveling Mercies
page 99

Chapter Ten: A Mother's Struggle
page 115

Chapter Eleven: Children Stories
page 125

Closing Remarks
page 137

Dedication

This gem in a book is dedicated to my loves, The Brown and Kimbrough families. I don't take for granted that I'm blessed to not only have my children, but to also have the beautiful extensions of family in my daughters and sons in laws, grandchildren, great-grandchildren, and great-great grandchildren to cherish this moment with me today. To my friends and spiritual family at church, along with my Pastor, and to all the ones who've paved the way for me, I hold you close to my heart and I want to personally say "thank you."

-Doris Norwilla Brown Kimbrough

Doris Kimbrough

Preface

As far back as I can remember, the sight of what gray hair meant to me use to make me sick! I chuckle as I think about this; there was a statement I use to constantly say behind old people's back as a little girl, *"you make me sick!"* I'm quite aware of how ugly that sounds; trust me when I tell you that my mother, Miss Janie Brown, help me to quickly recognize that type of behavior wouldn't be tolerated. I'm also glad God saw fit to help me understand the lessons I'd learned in life from those with gray hair on down to this very moment. When I look out in the world today, oh my… have the times changed. As a child, we were given little and made the most

PREFACE

out of what we had; nowadays you're given much and it's least appreciated. In my day, work ethic started at home. We had chores and worked hard for everything we got. These days the mentality seems to be you're entitled to any and everything you haven't earned. Our legs and mouth were the latest automobile, communication and newspaper. Today, technology has grown so much we now have Uber, city electric scooters, and my great-great granddaughters, both six years old, can teach me how to work my cellphone or laptop. In all these cases the gray hair played a vital role in keeping me grounded in not forgetting where I came from, what I've worked hard for and rightfully earned. But most importantly, I know what it really

PREFACE

means to survive and live a meaningful life at the tender age of ninety-five. Follow along as I share some secrets of my life with you.

CHAPTER ONE

Salem Hill

I'm Allergic to Gray Hair

Salem Hill

Who would have thought we'd see Winston Salem where it is today? The funny thing is most people in this town can quickly remember the Happy Hill area on the Southside of Winston Salem, NC. But for me, I have fond memories of growing up right across the street from Happy Hill in what was uncommonly known as Salem Hill. To speak of Salem Hill almost feels like it's taboo, as many people aren't around to tell the story of what it was like living back then. When I think about it, the part that sticks out in my mind is the hill. It was rightfully named Salem and Happy Hill because it rested on elevated land with plenty of nature and open space for the slaves to build and develop a community. Back in eighteen sixty-seven, the first black

I'm Allergic to Gray Hair

schoolhouse was built by the slaves for all black children to attend free in Forsyth County. Since there were no age requirements, parents were only responsible for getting their children to and from school. Back then, it was considered an honor to be able to learn to read and write and benefit not only yourself but others in your community too. Of course, decades later, as I was growing up, I developed a deep appreciation for that school. I got to attend it at the young age of five years old with my older cousins who were teenagers.

Today, the road commonly known as Waughtown Street was the dividing factor for the two sides of Happy and Salem Hill. Happy Hill was growing and becoming very prosperous that the blacks ended up populating across the street to keep building and established Salem Hill. In Salem Hill, I recall a community; *so close*, it was like your family. Our houses, often called "shotgun houses", weren't as nice as the ones on Main Street, but the people in our neighborhood were good people. Our houses resembled boxes, all piled up one on top of the other. By just standing near the front porch, you could see through the entire house to the backyard. When you opened the front door, it was just one huge open room that was usually sectioned off into three different areas of living. We would use curtains or whatever we saw fit to give some type of privacy for each section. Even though it looked like a tight space, still we had plenty

I'm Allergic to Gray Hair

of room. I know that sounds crazy, but we *really* made the best of it.

When I was a little girl, you didn't have to have a lot to make you happy. All you needed was good friends, good food and a decent place to stay. There really were no strangers in our neighborhood and people genuinely looked out for each other. If you were hungry or needed food, someone was always cooking and had extra food to feed others or give away. The community was full of industrious working people, always providing for and taking care of their families. If you needed a babysitter or someone to keep an eye on the kids, the neighbors would step in. Most families went to church regularly, and that was mostly every Sunday. Although we attended our own church in our community; we also attended the first and only historical black church in North Carolina that was built for slaves. In eighteen twenty-two, St. Philip Moravian Church was established for blacks. What could be preserved from that original church has been kept, but it's moved a few times and still stands today.

Happy and Salem Hill were continuing to grow. It was startling to watch our side of town eventually have its own school, theater, dance hall and a host of neighborhood businesses. Racism was thriving to its fullest potential. For clueless little children like me, racism was like that nagging mosquito that just wouldn't go away even though your mother

I'm Allergic to Gray Hair

sprayed you down with a repellent spray figuratively. That repellent spray that protected you growing up in those times mainly involved being obedient to the words of your parents and of course the gray-headed old folks I was allergic to and couldn't stand. They'd tell us to pray to God every day, don't stare at white people, and dare not open your mouth and speak or talk to them. It may sound ridiculous to you now, but for us, it was survival or be shot or killed instantly, no matter how young or old you were. But I was *always* a curious little girl, at times too curious and it cost me a lot. I needed to think for myself and always had a mind of my own. I had a question and an answer for everything! One time being curious took me somewhere I'd

Salem Hill

never been before.

CHAPTER TWO

The Highest Birthday Party

I'm Allergic to Gray Hair

The Highest Birthday Party

If it's one thing you'll always remember as a child, you never forget your first birthday party. All the kids in the neighborhood were at our house to celebrate with me. We had my party on a Saturday, mainly because most people worked during the week and that left Saturday and Sunday to do anything else. Around this time, RJ Reynolds Tobacco was popular in the city. I'll never forget, I had an aunt, who *loved* to chew tobacco. And I was a curious, might I add, nosey little girl. I was feeling excited and happy because it was *my* birthday. I had been watching my aunt just chew that tobacco and it seemed like she really was enjoying herself. I wondered; what would it taste like to me and would I like it too? I had already justified that, because it was my birthday, I deserved anything I wanted. The adults were in the kitchen preparing and getting things ready for the party. It was almost time for the other kids to come in, so we could get started. By the time they came in, I had already had a big wad of tobacco. The taste wasn't quite what I imagined; it had already started oozing out my mouth. This was on top of the fact that it was making me sick. I could see the facial expressions of some of the people; they thought it was blood and they were getting worried.

I remember somebody saying: *"What in the world is wrong with that child?"* I couldn't say or do much as I was high, sick to my stomach, and didn't know what to do. I took one glance at my birthday cake and it was

The Highest Birthday Party

over. I was so nauseas, I ended up vomiting all over my cake and in front of everyone present. That means all the neighborhood kids, my mother, aunt and all the other grown folks. As bad as I wanted to, I couldn't add tobacco to my list of things I was allergic to like old folks. I knew this result was because I was being hard headed, and had no business doing so. It didn't take long for me to figure out all things grown folks do, wasn't for me!

I survived the birthday party and gave all my friends something to laugh about and remember me by. My mother never let me live down what happened that day. Oddly enough, she could tell I suffered much guilt and embarrassment for what I had done, so she kindly skipped punishing me or

I'm Allergic to Gray Hair

whipping my backside. I'd be telling a lie if I told you that encounter was the only lesson I'd learned. It should have been enough, but I was too curious of a little girl to stop there. There was so much in life that I wanted to know, and I was determined to find out answers. My next truth or dare is a recap of what happened one time when I was thirsty.

The Highest Birthday Party

CHAPTER THREE

Colored Water

I'm Allergic to Gray Hair

Colored Water

G rowing up, there were many old folk sayings that we were told to help and protect us. Some of them didn't make sense as a kid, but nevertheless, during that time, a lot of things in life didn't add up. A famous one was: "*curiosity kills the cat.*" Being a young girl, quite a few things caught my attention. I took notice of how our houses in Salem Hill looked so different than the white people's houses my mother worked for. Our homes weren't fancy, as nicely decorated, or big in size. As we walked to town, stopping by to catch the lovely scent of Krispy Kreme Doughnuts near Old Salem was a favorite of mine. The people in there didn't mind giving us the doughnuts that were smashed or couldn't be sold to the public. There were certain

I'm Allergic to Gray Hair

restaurants, businesses and bathrooms for whites only. I quickly noticed two words associated with us as black people; "*negro* or *colored*." In my day, a lot of things weren't explained to children in details as to why it's this or that way. Out of respect and sometimes fear, you simply obeyed.

The more I think about it, these two words were everywhere to separate the blacks from the whites. It didn't take a genius to figure out we were frowned upon, especially by the looks they gave us and harsh words they'd say even in front of young children. The separate use for everything was as if we, as blacks, were the nagging mosquitos I talked about earlier that wouldn't go away. They even had separate water fountains for us to drink from. In the

Colored Water

back of a store we often visited, were two water fountains. One of course was for the whites; and there again, was the word "*negro*" on the other fountain for us. The lady in front of us was white and had her little girl with her to stop at the fountain. When I started to drink out of the fountain that said "*whites*", my mother almost had a hissy fit. She told me I couldn't drink from that fountain. I **immediately** wanted to know why. She said because it was for white people only. I thought to myself, "Ha! *White people only huh*?! *We'll see about that!*" I stepped back and slyly let my mother go in front of me. As she walked away and it was my turn next, I darted over to the white people fountain and got the biggest sip of water my juicy cheeks could hold and slowly gulped it down. I instantly looked around to see if anyone had seen me and no one did. So, I bent down again and got me another big sip and walked off.

I concluded that the water that said "*whites*" didn't taste any better or worse than the one that said "*negro.*" It crossed my mind, what was the big deal? It was a waste of time to have different fountains separating people and calling us ugly names. Throughout the years, I learned quite a bit about racism. But I do know one thing for sure, it can all be so simple. We, as humans, make it hard. It's difficult to digest how easily I could've been killed or taken away from my mother at that young age just because I took a sip of water. I think I might have

Colored Water

understood a little better if the water was artificially colored or tasted different. But the reality was clear in plain black and white, it wasn't. Water is water. That's a lot to think about, because at the end of the day, I'm still sipping colored water in some ways and to some people.

CHAPTER FOUR

God Accepts all Sinners

I'm Allergic to Gray Hair

In Salem Hill most folks were church goers, but there were a lot who didn't go to church. There was an empty house that men would go to and gamble. At the top of the hill, across the street, and along the path was the church I attended with my mother. There was nothing for anyone to be afraid of walking around in our neighborhood. It was much safer then, for children to cross the street to get to the store or church. As I'm walking, I could hear them laughing, shouting, and using bad words I was forbidden to say by my mother. But the moment they saw my little head coming around that corner they'd shout: "*Stop cursing! Here come Miss Janie Brown's daughter!*"

I used to have a favorite pocketbook

I'm Allergic to Gray Hair

that had a rooster on it. I took it everywhere with me. Even though I was headed to church, I was very curious as to what they'd be doing at that house. When I stopped by, they'd tell me to open my bag because they were going to give me some money to put in church. Every time they'd fill it up with all the change it could hold. There were dimes, nickels and quarters jiggling around in there. I would take that money and when it was time for offering, I'd open my bag and give all that money to church. I was so proud to do that for them.

One time, my older friends asked me why I put all that money in the offering like that. I told them because that's why they gave it to me, and I was doing what they asked. They told me I could put some of the money in church but not all of it. There was a store right across the path that had candy, soda, chewing gum, everything you'd think a child wanted to get their hands on. The older kids who could count well would count the money and separate what to put in church and left just enough for us all to buy what we wanted in the store. It didn't matter to me because the way I saw it, I was helping my friends and the men who gambled. But all that ended in due time.

One day, some of those older gray headed folks I'm allergic to caught wind of what was going on and told my mother. I got the worse spanking a little girl could imagine because I was crossing the street to go to the store during church service. The first thing came to my mind with those old folks was: "*you make me sick!*" But after that whipping, I knew never to cross that road again for anybody or anything!

Another time in church, being bored got the best of me. As kids whether you're real young or teenagers, all that's being said in church doesn't necessarily interest you and we knew better than to just get up and walk out. We knew to respect our parents, so we stayed. We were teenagers, my friends and I were sitting on the church benches inside. If you think of the benches at a park that's how the ones in church looked. Instead of listening to the Pastor preach, my friend's sister who was a little stout was sitting in front of us. This means quite much of her backside was hanging out between the openings on the bench. My friend said to me she bet I won't stick her sister. I told her of course I would. I asked her did she want me to stick her sister and if so, did she have a pin? She said she had a pin, and she gave it to me. Just as I had put the pin by her backside to stick her, the second thought came into my head that I shouldn't do this as we were already getting a lot of glares from the old gray headed folks sitting near us. Once I decided it's best not to do it, my friend pushed my hand and the pin went into her sister's bottom! I never seen anybody jump up so fast and shout the worst curse word you can think of in the Lord's house! I sat there straight faced and unbothered like I was clueless as to what had just

I'm Allergic to Gray Hair

happened. Now my friend didn't know any better, so she burst out laughing as it was quite funny to see. This made everyone believe that she was the one who did that to her sister. When church was out, that seem to be the talk of the whole service. I honestly wasn't about to admit that I did that. Once my friend realized she was about to get into serious trouble, she blurted out my name! My mother in complete shock said: *"she did what?!"* Surprisingly, I didn't get a whipping. As you can tell by now, my track record with spankings don't last long. It affected me for the moment, then I'm up to something else. I learned that day, parents know their children very well, even when you think they don't. Usually after church we can walk to the fairground with our friends and hang around while the rides were being set up. We just had to be home before it got dark. We got home from church and my mother let me get dressed, I had my own little money with me, and out the door I was planning on going. The children came by to get me, and my mother said: "*she's not going.*" My heart dropped, I just knew I hadn't heard her correctly! I broke down and cried, my friends tried to convince her, and she again not concerned at all, wouldn't change her mind. I will admit, that hurt my precious pride. I couldn't understand how my mom let me get dressed, made sure I had money, and just like that told me I couldn't go. I had no choice but to face the fact I had no business poking my friend.

I'm Allergic to Gray Hair

I learned a valuable lesson. Never let anyone talk me into doing something I knew I shouldn't be doing. I think about those men back then who didn't go to church or anyone else who didn't go. I think about the bad things we were doing in church, not paying attention at all. Now it's true, we were teenagers and kids, but we knew better. After that incident with sticking my friend, I did pray to God to forgive me. People have their reasons for why they believe in what they do. At that young age I understood that regardless God loved us all because we are sinners. If only we could keep that reasoning throughout life in dealing with people now. Somewhere along the lines we'll make mistakes. Would we want anyone to judge us? Those situations showed me God accepts all sinners and judging is up to him alone. Now, the effects of that spanking lasted a good while, until I was curious again.

CHAPTER FIVE

Working for Free

I'm Allergic to Gray Hair

Working for Free

When I think of how different the concept is instilled in children to work now, it's far different from when I was coming up. From a young age, children helped in the household chores and worked outside quite a bit. There wasn't any debate or begging us to help, we were told what to do and we did it, no questions asked. Well, except for me. I was always trying to find a way around what needed to be done. Being an only child, it was just me and my mother to care for everything. I had a good friend who would come over almost every day. She came from a large family, so I know she was happy to come by and eat with me and help me do my chores before we'd go outside to play. My mother didn't mind me fixing us food long as we ate all of it and never wasted it. You didn't just do what you wanted to do, there was a routine you'd follow faithfully each day before starting the chores.

As I mentioned earlier in chapter one, we lived in what was called "shotgun houses." That means the house was straight through, a small front porch and no back porch. There were no bathrooms back then. If you had to use the bathroom, we had what was called a "nightjar" that was kept in the house, that could be used for doing number one (urinate) not number two (stool). If you had to do number two, no matter what time it was, you had to go outside and sometimes you might could get someone to go with you. The first thing we'd do in the morning was dump that jar out in the toilet outside, rinse it out with water, then place it in the sun so the heat would hit it and minimize the smell.

The next thing you'd do was make your bed up. You never wanted anyone to come to your house and it's dirty and your bed isn't made. Once that's done you can start any of the other chores either before you'd eat or afterwards. Since my friend always came by, I'd fix our food and let her eat all the food she wanted because I knew she didn't get as much as she'd like at home and we were helping each other. After we were done eating, we'd get to the chores.

Our biggest chore we had was to wash clothes. Let me be very clear, there was no washing machine, dryer, or laundry mat to do so. It required three big tubs of water that you had to go outside to fetch. The first tub was the wash water that you'd wash the clothes in. The second tub was the rinse water, where you washed most of the suds out with. The third tub was also rinse water, however we had something that was called "bluing" we'd add to the third tub of water that helped preserve the coloring of clothes including white clothes. We had a big iron skillet we used to heat boiling water up by the fire we made with wood. You'd wash in the first tub, rinse in the next, rinse in the last tub and final rinse with boiling water in the skillet to be sure the clothes were completely cleaned before hanging on the clothes line outside.

Let me remind you, the clothes had to be washed every day. I had washed two days in a row and I was not feeling like washing the clothes, so I skipped the boiling water step. I went to hang the clothes on the line and some of them old gray headed folks was walking by and talking about how dirty the clothes were on the line. They commented that if they were Miss Janie Brown, they'd make me wash them over. I could hear mother was coming in the house, so I rushed and tried to get the clothes in before she came out. She must have known what I had done because she told me to just go eat and she'd get them. When she brought them in, she didn't put them away as normal, instead she let them hit the floor. My jaw dropped in disbelief! She punished me by making me wash them all over again and my friend wasn't allowed to

I'm Allergic to Gray Hair

help me. I fussed and I cried and fussed some more. I slept great that night, but I was so upset that she'd make me do all that again and alone at that. The next day I was determined I'd fix her.

That morning, I decided I didn't want to do any chores. My friend seemed worried because she asked me what did I mean? I told her I didn't feel like doing anything and will do it later but for now we're going to the field and play. She asked what if Miss Janie Brown came back. I told her she's not coming home because she can't get off until three o'clock. It didn't matter to me because I was going to play. Once we got to the field, one of the kids told me Miss Janie Brown was home. I told them they didn't know what they were talking about because she's at work. Another child came and told me the same thing. By this time, I was getting irritated because I knew she was at work, but this was starting to worry me. I figured we'd head back and come through the back door to see if she was home. Sure enough, she was sitting on the front porch.

I tried to jump right into doing the chores, and to my surprise she told me to get a bucket of water to wash the clothes. She used to say *"Hun, that's all you got to do, get one last bucket of water hun."* I went out the back and was still mad that I had to wash these clothes another day, so I started mimicking her. I wasn't allergic to my mother but that day she made me sick too! Here I am in the back yard going off. I had my hands on my hips and

I'm Allergic to Gray Hair

stomped around. Just as I uttered *"you make me sick"* ready to start my chant over again, my feet left the ground and Miss Janie Brown had me dangling in the air! She put me across her knees and wore my backend out for all I had done but most importantly for disobeying and disrespecting her. I can say for a minute, I thought my mother cured me of my allergies with old folks because I had the scars to remind me of that spanking. But as usual, it lasted for a while, then something else would come along and make me curious.

It's safe to say I tested her patience. Most children these days don't even realize how good they have it. The things mentioned above was an everyday list of chores. Getting the water wasn't an easy task. I eventually

Working for Free

got some of the neighborhood kids to help me get water and I paid them some coins. People take for granted all they have access to today. You don't have to step outside to use the bathroom every time. You don't have to go up the hill to get water to fill all three tubs and the skillet to wash clothes in. Most of us now have a washer and dryer in our home. Getting to go outside and play was a privilege. There were no cellphones, tablets, or laptops. We were each other's company and we were closer too. Those hard lessons of how to properly do this or that chore made me appreciate it more. We didn't have access to all the abundance we do today, but our homes were always neat and clean. Our clothes fresh; free of dirt and odors. Many of us made a living off keeping people clothes washed, dried and folded. We surely didn't have much but we made the best of it. Therefore, it was all free lessons that were worth working for.

CHAPTER SIX

Stand for Something or Fall for Anything

I'm Allergic to Gray Hair

Stand for Something or Fall for Anything

I often hear people say what they would have done if they were being raised in my day. If it were them, they would have done this. The truth of the matter is we did what was best for us during that time. I think of my mother growing up, a strong woman, single and raising me by herself. No matter what people did in our neighborhood, whether it be bootlegging, gambling, some drugs back then, everyone respected her. People including myself also knew Miss Janie Brown didn't play. She was a woman of few words with deep purpose as a lot of people looked up to her. I remember everyone didn't always agree with some of the people my mother was nice to and helped. She always told me to treat people with respect but have dignity about yourself. She never allowed what others murmured about to dictate how she treated someone.

I remember one of her friends was the lady who had a liquor house and sold whiskey. She was considered the bootlegger of the neighborhood. I didn't know what any of this meant being a girl. The lady had a little baby and my mother told me to go to her house to get the clothes for her to wash. She strictly told me, for many reasons, never go inside the house. I went to this lady's home, and she opened the door to hand me the clothes. As usual, my curiosity always struck at the wrong time, so I asked her could I have some water. She told me sure and to come inside while she gets it. I cautiously walked in feeding my interest as I looked around and took in the view from this house that everybody talked about. To keep her distracted and to see more, I asked could I see her baby. She said sure and guided me to another room. Just then we heard a car door shut and a loud disturbing pounding at the door. She calmly said it was the police. I got so scared; all I could think of was my mother told me not to go inside and here I am about to go to jail from being at the whiskey lady's house. She told me to take the baby and sit down, be quiet and say nothing. Out of being nervous and frightened I told her I had to go. She sternly told me I wasn't going anywhere yet but to tend to the baby and she placed the bag of dirty clothes near me. She had a stool that she put by the kitchen sink and

I'm Allergic to Gray Hair

her oldest little girl climbed up there and started emptying all the whiskey down the drain. There was a woman who was in the kitchen that joined her as she started rinsing out the jars to get rid of the smell. She opened the door and the police barged in as if they were looking for something. One officer said: *"I see you got rid of your evidence."* She was cursing the police out I was so scared I could have wet my pants. I just knew he would shoot her in front of us. She asked him did he see any evidence, in which he told her he could smell it. She then told him what he could do with his smell and where to shove it. He turned and looked at me and asked what was I doing there? I told him I came to get the clothes so I can wash. He told me to get them and get out of here! I ran out that door so fast like my life depended on it and never looked back!

When I got home my mother asked me what took me so long. I told her I got thirsty and wanted a drink of water, but the police came, and I had to stay until they left. She told me, no that's not right, she knew I was being nosey and went inside the house. She told me the next time she tells me something to do and what not to do and I disobey her, she'll give me a whipping I'll never forget! I nodded my head in complete agreement, I never wanted to visit that memory again.

Sometime later in life, this same dear friend of my mother's whom she used to wash clothes for was killed. I don't know who or why, but in her

I'm Allergic to Gray Hair

line of work, someone stabbed her to death. It was explained to me that I could go to her funeral, but our friend wouldn't be waking up. I was told it'll be the last time I'd see her, but she'll be dressed up and seem as if she was sleeping. My mother was at work and told my cousin to get me dressed for the funeral. She didn't get me dressed and long story short, I ended up not being able to go to the funeral because my mother couldn't wait for me. I thought my life was over and I cried uncontrollably. No one could stop me from crying or cheer me up. It didn't make any sense to me as to why I couldn't see my friend as it was going to be the last time. I was so hurt, and I still remember that to this day. As a child, all I could understand was she was my mother's friend even though she ran a business that was frowned upon. She was the nicest lady you'd meet and was always there for us as we were for her and her children. Now I would never get to see her again, although my mother begged me to try to remember her the way she was. I'm still holding tight of those memories of her as that's all I have, and I know she's in a better place now.

There was even a time during summer break I went with my mother to the white family house she cleaned for. Their daughter was my best friend and I was hers. My friend and her mother had shown us plenty of times how much they cared for and respected my mother and me even though we were black. A feeling of self-worth

I'm Allergic to Gray Hair

sparked inside me that I'll never forget. One day we were playing in the garage with our toys and having fun. She had a little white girl over to play with us that lived in her neighborhood. She too was happy to see me and didn't call me ugly names like they called most black people in our city. They didn't mind touching my hand, and hugging me, or eating with me. We'd play dress up with our dolls and play in each other's hair pretending to be someone famous or rich. Suddenly a car pulled up in the drive way and a white man jumped out running towards us. I was kind of scared but also curious as he wasn't my friend's father. He grabbed the other little white girl and was jerking her away from us. He looked at me, breathing heavily and hard as if he'd seen a ghost and demanded to know why was I there? Why was I playing with them? He called me the horrible name white people said that I'd heard so much whenever we came into town. My friend jumped up and told him not to call me that! Her mother must have heard the commotion and quickly came to the garage. He then turned his rage towards her as my mother stood to the side calm as always but standing boldly without a sign of fear in her eyes. I was devastated and angry at the same time. I didn't understand much and especially this color thing. I was hurt that he thought I was an animal trying to attack his daughter. We all were just little girls playing together. They say the apple don't fall too far from the tree and I knew exactly

I'm Allergic to Gray Hair

where my friend got her feistiness and boldness from. Her mother told him to never use those words again and to get off her property! I could tell she too was a woman of her dignity by the fearlessness she had in her eyes!

What took place next is what you call a real moment of silence. Our mothers grabbed and hugged us like no one else mattered in the world. They didn't say a word but the way they caressed, comforted and assured us let us know we were protected and didn't have to fear anyone. Afterwards, our mothers left to go back inside the house. I must admit, I was still feeling bad and didn't have much confidence after that. It's hard to register that much hatred could be inside of a person to show towards a child. I'll never forget what my friend did. She told me how she knew I felt bad, but I'm old enough to understand that you can't pay attention to everything a person says or calls you. She said it was time for me to know it's nobody in the world that is better than I am, and no one that I'm better than. We all are the same and we just have different skin colors. She told me she wanted to show me something. She went and got a pin and told me to stick my hand out. She stuck me with the pin and for a minute I thought I'd have to smack her for sticking me because it hurt. Then she stuck herself and reminded me that we both bleed red. She said her great grandmother had slaves and she had respect for them and always taught them to read and write. She taught her family to respect them too and gave them land and money. She wanted me to remember one thing, I am a beautiful girl and one day I'll be a very strong woman when I grow up. I made a promise to her that I'd always believe in myself and stand up for myself. She spoke to me with such conviction I believed her and knew what she was telling me was true.

That day has always marked a changing point in my life for me. Sometimes we don't know who that person will be to speak life into us. The person that will make us believe in ourselves unlike ever before. For me, especially as a child, that person was my white friend. She taught me white people weren't superior to me. I believed it so much it almost got me in trouble or killed sometimes but I stood strong on believing it. We continued to keep in touch throughout the years. We grew up to marry and have children of our own and although she's no longer on this earth, I'll always treasure our friendship as she taught me how important it was to stand up for myself or fall for anything.

Miss Janie Brown holding great-grandson Ronald Gray

CHAPTER SEVEN

Mother's Day for the Motherless

I'm Allergic to Gray Hair

Mother's Day for the Motherless

It seemed to be one lady who was older that I feel cured me of old gray headed folks making me sick. By this time, I'm grown and have a few children of my own. She was a sweet Christian woman who lived in our community ever since I was a little girl, and strangely enough, I really liked her. We attended the same church and even though she told my mother everything that I did, I still had so much love for her. One day, around the last of April, I was walking by her house and had a shawl wrapped around my shoulders. I was headed to see another friend of mine who stayed close by on another street. We both chatted about how cold it was, and she told me she loved my shawl. I told her I'd make her one for Mother's Day.

I'm Allergic to Gray Hair

By the time I got back home from visiting my friend, I honestly had forgotten about making her a shawl. I didn't think about it anymore until that Saturday, the day before Mother's Day. I panicked as it was kind of late in the evening after four thirty, and most stores were closing. I didn't drive or had a car and none of my children stayed close by either. I called my friend whom I'd visited earlier, and asked her nephew to take me to the store to buy the material. He did and I got the prettiest white material where you could pull the thread apart and make the edges fringe for a classy look. Saturday evening, I cooked my dinner as I usually do before going to church that next morning. It was getting late after eleven o'clock that night and I

Mother's Day for the Motherless

was still working on the shawl. I finally finished at four a.m. Sunday morning. I got up and wrapped it in a beautiful gift tissue with a card I wrote for her saying Happy Mother's Day. I headed towards her house to take the shawl to her. I was about to knock on the door until something divine caught my eye through her window. I could hear her praying out loud. What she said I'll never ever forget:

"Lord I know this is Mother's Day, and you never gave me any children. But you gave me so many other folks children, and I thank you for it. On this day, I'm asking you to be a mother and a father to me, and even though I don't have any children, just let me feel like a mother. Lord you took my husband and my sister and my nephew, *so I don't have anybody. But Lord I still thank you for everything you've done and given me. But for today, I ask you to help me make it through as you always do, Amen."*

At this moment, I was filled with every emotion I wasn't prepared for. All I could think of was, what a wonderful thing to thank God for the things you do have. Even though you long for other things, still be grateful for what you do have. I tried to get my little face straightened up so I could knock on her door. As I knocked, she came to the door and took notice of my face and how messed up I was. She asked what was wrong. I told her nothing, I just came to bring her shawl. She cried and hugged me and we both cried together. I never told her I heard her prayer. Taking the time to make that shawl was the best thing I have ever done because it brought me so much joy.

That shawl taught me many things. Always thank God for what you do have and take nothing for granted even when you feel you're without. It taught me to appreciate the gift in being able to have children and experience one of the greatest joys of a woman, being a mother. As bad as it may sound, I'm glad I forgot to make the shawl until the last minute as I might have missed hearing that beautiful prayer. Sometimes, we have things that are simple to us but mean everything to someone else. Standing there hearing every word of that prayer help me to appreciate the importance of checking

I'm Allergic to Gray Hair

on people too. She once was one of those old gray headed folks I couldn't stand, but in her own way, she was looking out for and protecting me. She was fulfilling her role of longing to be a mother. This was confirmation of what we've all heard numerous times, "it takes a village to raise a child." She too was part of that village for me. When you think about it, when was the last time you could say you heard someone's prayer? If you did, would you view them differently? Would you have a better understanding of who they are? That day was placed in my life for a reason as I had much to learn about the folks, I called myself allergic to.

CHAPTER EIGHT

Get Off the Bus

I'm Allergic to Gray Hair

Get Off the Bus

I remember when I was a teenager with a few of my friends, we had a bus situation. This was during a time again where racism was at its highest. Black people had to sit at the back of the bus, it didn't matter if the bus was empty or full, you couldn't sit in the front. The front was for white people only. My friends and I were coming from the movies and took the bus home. On one stop a few white girls around our age got on the bus. Instead of them staying up front like they were supposed to, as it was their privilege they came to the back of the bus. This meant we had to crowd up on the very last seat of the bus to respect them. It was very cramped and not big enough for a lot of people, but we had to obey

I'm Allergic to Gray Hair

the law. To make matters worse, one of my friends was a very stout girl and she could have taken up that area by herself so that she's comfortable. Just imagine us all at the back of the bus on the last seat along with my friend, until our stop came up.

We all know children are notorious for doing what they're not supposed to do when their parents aren't around. My friend who was a big girl was also the biggest dare devil of all. I never could figure out if she meant to do it or it was an accident but either way it was another lesson learned. My friend loved to smoke, which you know she never did in front of her parents. As she lit a cigarette to smoke, one of the white girls in front of us hair caught on fire. She was twitching and turning in her seat trying to put the fire out. We were trying to help her too. The bus driver kept looking back there trying to see what was going on, but he couldn't drive and watch us at the same time. We all finally put the fire out and my friend sternly told those girls if they tell it, she was going to get her off the bus and take her somewhere and hang her. The girls promised they'd never tell anyone and each time we saw each other in passing from time to time we'd just stare at each other. The lesson in that was sometimes laws are in place for a reason to protect us. I think you've read enough to know I wasn't scared of much, was a dare devil myself at times, but when I think of how bad that could have been, it's an eye opener. Was it necessary for them to come all

I'm Allergic to Gray Hair

the way to the back of the bus to sit when the bus was pretty much empty to choose a seat? Of course, this meant the further back whites came to sit on the bus, blacks would have to move to the very back and crowd up. No, this young lady didn't deserve to get her hair caught on fire, but it certainly makes you think; would anything had happened if we all were sitting where we were supposed to be?

I'm sure everyone remembers Rosa Parks's story of her riding the bus and the historical moment that went down in history for her opposing to be treated that way. Well it becomes very real when I recall my own incidents within my precious city of Winston Salem, NC. The one I'll never forget is one evening my bus ride home after a long day. Black people still had to sit at the back of the bus. And when no one was on the bus, if the two seats right behind the steps were available, we could sit there. Again, this is only if no whites were on the bus. If the seats were full, we had to stand up. I had just had some teeth extracted and decided I'd go to work anyway. I was a sitter for this little white girl. At first, I didn't feel any pain but later in the afternoon, as the temperatures dropped outside, the pain settled in swiftly. All the feeling started to come back into my face and the pain was excruciating. I took this job because it wasn't far from my house and I could usually walk. But this day, I was in so much pain I could barely walk. I'm not

I'm Allergic to Gray Hair

sure if you've ever had a tooth ache before but it's the worst pain you could ever imagine. I decided to take the bus as I knew it was coming soon and that would get me out the cold. When the bus came, the driver opened the door for me to get on, and it was only two little older white ladies on the bus. They seemed very nice and cordial, so I took the seat directly behind the steps as the pain was starting to settle in again from my tooth ache. I knew I couldn't afford to pass out and not walk in front of these white people and expect them to help me as a black woman. I made it to the seat directly behind the steps.

The bus driver stopped the bus and said: *"Get up and get on the back seat."*

One of the white ladies said: *"It's nobody on the bus, why would she need* to get up and go to the back?"

He said: "*Because I said so, and that's where all negros go to fill up the bus at.*"

I didn't move, I sat there, then he stopped the bus again.

He said: "*I guess you heard me, you supposed to be on the back seat of this bus.*"

I got up, paused, got off the bus, then turned to him and said: "*I'll walk home and freeze to death before I sit on the back of that bus.*"

I walked home, as it was a couple of blocks from where I was at. Everything was racing through my mind during this time. Why are we still dealing with this racist mess? Where is the respect for a woman period no matter the color of her skin? If they only knew the pain I was in during that time. All this frustration, anger, hurt, and agony from being sick, set my emotions on high. Tears escaped my eyes but instantly froze like icicles once my tears met the chilling temperatures that evening. I made it home and can't describe the physical state I was in. Pain was shooting everywhere all over my body as I think back on this story, I'd do it all over again if I had to, to stand in my right to not be treated in such a way as a human being. Someone else may read this and disagree and feel it was only one time, but for me that day, in all that pain, I was determined not be in the back of the bus where the air and wind creeps in more to poison my tooth ache just because I'm black and sitting at the back of the bus is where they said I belong. These stories could mean so little to the average person now, but in our day, it could make you or break you. You had to decide what you could live with in the consequences. I've seen some change today with racism but a lot of it still lingers on strong. That's why I compared it to a nagging mosquito that just won't let go. We must ask ourselves today; are we still living by the same repellents so to speak that was taught to my generation? What are we doing about our rights? Do we know when the time is to speak up and when it's time to be silent? I encourage you to think about that the next time you get on or off a bus? How easy was it for you, or have you forgotten?

I'm Allergic to Gray Hair

CHAPTER NINE

Traveling Mercies

I'm Allergic to Gray Hair

S pending so much time in the church growing up opened the doors for a lot of things once I was grown. I may not have known everything but if it's two things I knew; I loved the Lord and I loved to sing! Getting together to sing was such a normal thing for us that we ended up forming a famous gospel group in the nineteen sixties in our area. We had five original members including myself. We sang and traveled together for thirty years performing all up and down the coast and back. We recorded songs and the beautiful part is each one of us could sing, but lord put us together and it was over! There's so much to being in a group traveling and, singing, that most people aren't aware of. It's not easy being in a recording

I'm Allergic to Gray Hair

group, you have different personalities to adjust to and schedule conflicts, personal life, etc. For us we had a few things solid in place as to how long we lasted. We always prayed before each show together, settled our differences quickly, and respected each other no matter what.

I know for myself how hard it was on my family as I was a single mother and had nine children. My mother Miss Janie Brown helped me out a lot, along with my older children stepping in to care for their younger siblings while I was gone. Somehow, the Lord made it work for all of us to continue to get the support we needed in caring for our families, while being on the road. I look at television today and some things are familiar to me. All most people see is the performance but it's so much behind the scenes they don't see. We had so many bloopers or things that went wrong or not according to plans. I can recall a time our custom robes were forgotten, and we had to borrow robes from the church whom we were performing for. One time one of the ladies in the group was so in the spirit she slid off the bench by the piano and hit the floor! We carried on as if nothing had happened and played it off like it was a part of the routine. When we got back to the dressing room, we fell out laughing! We had times were the devil was determined to intervene again and in the middle of catching the spirit one of the lady's wig came flying off and flew through the window. If you could see everybody trying to catch that wig before it got out the window. The only part was, she forgot to comb her hair before putting it on. We quickly made a curtain like around her to distract the audience and helped her get her wig back on. I reminded her, as women we love to change up and try new things. I personally changed wigs every two weeks or so. But I always had my hair braided down, plenty of bobby pins in place, so I could throw my head back, or anything and that wig wasn't coming off! My motto then and still is today, secure the wig! After that one time, she never had that problem again!

One time I circled back to my old ways of growing up, speaking my mind when I probably should have been quiet! While on the road traveling to Delaware, one of the ladies was going on and on about her having to perform at a funeral every day of the week. The rest of us kind of looked at each other like whatever since nobody believed that. I mean think about it, that's a lot of people dead for you to sing at their funerals every day of the week?! Well I said that out loud and it didn't set well with her. We had a heated debate about it, and I had heard enough so I asked her what did she want to do about it? We can pull over and fight and handle this. Our driver was so disappointed in us he kept telling us don't act like that and just squash it. I told him to pull over because I was tired of hearing her mouth. It was getting to be dusk dark and we were in the country. I could tell she was heated and ready to go. I hollered at him to stop that car and he did. She jumped right out the car! I rolled my window down and told her how stupid she looked standing in those woods. I told her we out in the middle of nowhere and a bear will come out and grab her and we'll be getting right on down the road without her! She stopped and looked at me and said I was the craziest grown woman she'd ever seen in her life! She was so pissed at me but knew we had to laugh at the same time. Everybody laughed so hard because she jumped out the car ready to fight!

We had some of the best times together. Often when you're remembering those good times, the unexpected memories surface too. Amazingly, out of all those years of traveling, we never had anything drastic or depressing happen to us. I've always believed someway and somehow, God always has a way of showing you that something would happen soon. We had one performance that just didn't add up to us. It was a normal church anniversary performance and for some reason everyone at that church was in the spirit, crying, and full of emotion like we'd never see each other again. We all hugged and cried and hugged some more. It was time for us to rest as we had a full day, and everyone was exhausted from all the crying and singing we'd done. One of the girls always used to mess with me as I was the oldest and she got in the bed laying up under me like she was my little girl. I fussed and told her get up I don't have any children here all my babies are home! She just laughed at me as she thought I was something else too. But we all ended up getting some rest to prepare to go home that next morning. Normally we're laughing, joking, singing, just cutting up and having a good time. But it was the total opposite, nobody was laughing at all. Something was wrong and we felt it, but nobody knew how to address it or call it. Later that night at the church, someone prepared a ham for us to eat. My friend who was like a daughter to me and had crawled up next to me that night before, sliced the ham for us to eat. It was the weirdest thing to explain but I have never in my life seen a ham sliced so perfect and each slice laid as if it wasn't attached to the bone. I looked around the room to see if anyone had noticed this. It was just my son and I who later discussed it on our way home how strange that was. I'm sure someone would think it's just a ham that was carved. But to us it was more, and we just didn't know why.

That Monday I called to check in with everybody to see if they rested well. I called my friend, my kid daughter so to speak of our group to tell her about a Christmas play we were invited to. She said she didn't want to go to the play for all she know she might not be here at Christmas. It didn't bother me at that time, but I thought afterwards maybe she knew something. I told her if she's here I'll tell the people we'll be there, so she said okay. Later I realized I told her the wrong date and called her back. The person who answered

I'm Allergic to Gray Hair

the phone almost made me think I'd dialed the wrong number. This man said he was Lieutenant such and such, so I told him I'm sorry I have the wrong number. Again, I hung up and called back, and he said the same thing, so I asked if this is the residence of my friend. He told me it was her residence and she wouldn't be coming to the phone. I told him thank you and I hung up. I immediately called her sister to tell her what this man said and to see if everything is alright. As I asked her was something going on, the piercing screams she did answered what I feared. She told me my friend had just been killed by her boyfriend. We found out right after that my friend had made her mind up that she couldn't live the life she wanted to live with her boyfriend staying with her. To be a person who's singing gospel songs, have her life in order and lead others to Christ, she couldn't carry on this way. She loved serving the Lord and singing to him and traveling the road with us. These things made her truly happy. They got into a terrible argument about this, and she turned to get some of his clothes to put him out, he started stabbing her to death. A lot of her stabs were in her back, as it was later revealed. The extent to how he mutilated her is demonic to recall. He stabbed her beyond anger to the point that he cut out and butchered certain feminine parts of her body. As if this wasn't inhumane enough, he did so in the presence of her young son who managed to escape next door to alert the neighbors to call the police.

Even in closing my eyes today to speak of this is so painful. It was the hardest thing for us as a group to accept. No one deserves to be crucified in such a manner! She was our sister, our friend, a mother, daughter, and gifted spirit within our community. We all have had so many of our loved ones pass in death, but NEVER to the degree of how she was ripped from our hearts. We couldn't help but recall that last night together, we had no drive to laugh and cut up like we normally did, we just cried and hugged each other. In some strange way we were grieving her early. Within a few days, abruptly she was taken from us. I still hear the screams of her sister on the phone when I called her. The wails in our cries as a group trying to understand why and longing to embrace our friend again.

From that moment on, everything changed as nothing was the same. It was unbearable pain to try to carry on when a huge portion of us was missing. I still have my days of trying to work through the agony of losing someone so close to me. I'm grateful for the thirty years we had together to make so many memories with. We sung and made some powerful songs for the Lord and those are the memories I choose to hold on to. As we traveled, there was mercy all around us in ways we can't describe.

I'm Allergic to Gray Hair

CHAPTER TEN

A Mother's Struggle

I'm Allergic to Gray Hair

A Mother's Struggle

Life dealt me quite a few challenges while raising my family. Even though my husband wasn't there as he had left and was in another state with someone else, I was determined to raise my children and we were going to make it. Being a single mother or father is one of the most fulfilling roles in life. I always worked and had quite a few jobs to support us. I also made pretty good money back then too. I worked so much, it took a toll on my body. By the time I paid rent, utilities and groceries for my large family, it was a lot to handle. Rent back then was around five dollars a week, which adds up to be twenty -five dollars a month. It seems like nothing but it's a lot when you have a lot of children like I did.

I'm Allergic to Gray Hair

I worked myself so much, I ended up in the hospital. My doctor called social service and cursed them out. He told them I've always worked. Based off the money I made after all my bills and feeding my children it's not enough. He told them if I were white this wouldn't be an problem. The lady from social service came out when I got home and had my gas on and gave me vouchers for food which is like food stamps. They also paid a few more bills, so it all worked out. I could have dwelled on the fact that they denied me a few times when I went down there. But the impact my doctor had on them was what counted. I really needed that help then and God saw fit to use my doctor to get it done. That was a blessing and I couldn't have been more grateful.

A Mother's Struggle

One time I was waiting, for my check to come so we could get food and supplies for the house. Usually I could make it until the check came but this time, I was completely out of everything and had no food. One thing I did was always talk to my children and let them know what's going on. I was so disappointed because I didn't know what to do. I went and laid down but before doing so, I said a prayer to God. Later I heard a knock at the door, and it was my neighbor who said she had something for me so come to her house. I told the kids I'd be right back. I went to her house and she had so much food for me. She said she had cleaned out her fridge and wanted to make sure she got that food to us because she knew we could use it.

I'm Allergic to Gray Hair

Another time I was short on rent and didn't have the money for it. I again had a check coming soon but it wasn't coming fast enough to take care of what I needed. I prayed pouring my heart out to the Lord and saying how I'd been feeling. After that I went to lay down and one of the boys yelled the mail came. He said it was an envelope from New York. It turns out it was a small child support check from the state of New York where they got my husband and made him send a payment. It was exactly fifty dollars and I needed twenty-five for rent and still had another twenty-five to buy groceries and provide for my children.

The fondest memory was I absolutely had no money for food another time.

A Mother's Struggle

The bread was out and everything else we had. I told my children our situation and told them they could lay down to rest, but I was going to figure it out after I prayed. I took a can of tomatoes out of the cabinet and opened it to try to feed each of the children a little bit. As I emptied the can I heard a clink. I looked and on the plate was a quarter. I couldn't believe it and I sent one of the kids to the store to buy a loaf of bread.

I could go on and on about being a single mother. To be honest that by itself is another book! But the most important thing I take from being a mother is the sacrifices you must make for your babies. Sometimes it gets so hard and all you know is these babies

I'm Allergic to Gray Hair

are looking to you for the answer. They're relying on you to make a miracle happen. In those moments you quickly realize it's not about you and it's solely not you who makes it happen. You must have total trust and faith in the Lord. You must believe that it will work out and it will, if you believe! Have a few friends who support you and will be there for you. I always had this one friend that I could rely on in times of need. We both checked with each other first before anyone else to see how we could help each other. Keep your children in the know too with what's going on. You'll be shocked at how well children understand and handle challenges better than adults do. I would do it all again if I had to for my children and I only can hope

A Mother's Struggle

they can appreciate the sacrifices I've made for them so we can be here today.

CHAPTER ELEVEN

Children's Stories

I'm Allergic to Gray Hair

It's always been said that you reap what you sow. I know me being a handful for my mother and all the others who helped raised me would come back on me somewhere in my children. I was blessed to have nine children and here's some of my fond memories of them growing up for each child.

Doris: She was a very good child and beyond smart. She was younger than the boys, but she'd tie their shoes and get them ready. They always looked up to her because she was in charge. Doris would let them do things without telling on them, but if they made her mad, she'd tell on them. The bus line was a pretty good walk from our house, but she had a friend that after the football games she'd walk with

I'm Allergic to Gray Hair

her home. There was a hangout spot everyone went to that had games and they'd dance, etc. Everybody always thought Doris was such a good child, while all the other children were out and stopping at this place Doris was coming home and her friend would walk her home. I didn't know until one day recently we were talking about this young lady, her friend. Doris told how everybody always thought they were so good, because they didn't go to the spot to hang out. What they did was go before everyone else and played all they wanted that by the time the other kids came they were leaving. So, I never knew this all these years until Doris was grown and telling the story one day. She had a mind of her own!

Denise: She was the baby of my

children and was around five years old for this story. Everybody loved Denise, she was the spoiled child of the gang. She pretty much got what she wanted. This Sunday I was singing on the choir and Doris was watching Denise trying to keep her calm as she was getting restless from being in church awhile. She was ready to go home now and didn't want to wait until church got out. Doris told her we were going in a minute just be quiet and wait. I was on the choir so I could see them good. Denise was determined to get up and go home now so she got mad and slapped Doris. I could hear that smack from the stage. I didn't wait until service was over, I got off the stage and got my children to head home and asked Doris did Denise smack her? She was so upset

I'm Allergic to Gray Hair

and trying to keep her cool and said Denise did smack her. I got my switch and tore her behind up for smacking her sister. After Denise calmed herself down from her whipping, she decided to go next door and tell my neighbor what I had done to her and showed her legs. Then my neighbor had the nerve to come to my house and ask me did I whip Denise? I told her if she doesn't get out of here, she's going to get one too! My neighbor took Denise and off they went back to her house! She often thought Denise was her child, but she couldn't save her that day!

Doris Kimbrough Evans

Denise Kimbrough Gillis

Lawrence: Lawrence is my oldest child. He spent most of his life with his father's side of the family in Boston, Massachusetts then later relocated to New York. He would visit us in North Carolina sometimes.

Leslie: Oh, I never had any trouble out of my dear Leslie! He was always trying to learn and willing to teach you too. He was so into his books, looking for something to research or follow up on. Leslie was always a helpful person, willing to do what he could for people.

Alford Lee Sr.: He was my "do my own thing" child. My mother, Miss Janie Brown used to make homemade wine. She taught me how to make it too and from time to time, I'd let the children taste it. No one could get it by themselves. But Alford Lee, he'd sneak and get the wine and drink it all then try to put water there to replace it. Another time, he had his friends he'd went to school with, so they'd ride the bus acting as if they were going to school. I'd get a call from the principal saying he's calling about our boy, it's been a little over a week and the school hasn't seen Alford Lee. Long story short, he was skipping school to go gamble with his friends.

Michael: Michael was such a good and smart child. When he was in school, he had to have a few lessons with speech to help him pronounce some words better. They'd send a teacher out to the house to help him and I'd talk him through his words, so he'd feel comfortable. It turned out to be very helpful for him and he excelled all throughout school and college. Now it's like who doesn't know Dr. Kimbrough as we call him! Mr. Cool!

Gregory: When the children were young, we moved from Salem Hill to Happy Hill. There was a small heater in one of the bedroom closets that the kids knew was off limits. They were not allowed to touch it unless given permission. One day I smelled something burning so I ran to see what it was. One of my children had messed with the heater and cut it on, and the closet was full of clothes. The fire hadn't started quite yet but it was on its' way, as the clothes in the closet were scorched. I got my belt and I told Gregory I knew two things: it was him and he knew better. I hadn't even hit him yet, I just had the belt in my hand getting in motion to hit him and he shouted: *"Oh Lord Jesus please don't! Stop! Don't hit me!"* Not one tear in sight! I couldn't even go any further. I turned and walked out before he could see me because I was so tickled as I recalled doing these same things to my mother. Gregory was my payback child, I always knew what he was up to and doing, as he mirrored me in my mischievous ways a lot.

Charles: He was another smart one. He'd go into town with his brothers, and when people were selling the shopping bags, he'd stand there and smile at the ladies and rarely say much. The people would stop and say how cute he was and give him all this change. When the boys came home from working in town, Charles would usually have the most money out of everybody. He was younger but he watched and observed very well! A charming personality!

Bobby: Bobby was a pretty good child. The only thing with him was he like to smoke behind my back. What children don't know is cigarettes have a scent, so you can smell it. I would tell him if you're going to smoke, you better buy your own cigarettes. If you can't buy them, then you can't smoke. When he got a little older, he'd go with most of the guys into town and shine shoes to have some change of their own. Later, they'd go to the golf course and caddy. Bobby would always find a way to do what he wanted. He believed in working to do for himself. I'm sure you figured out by now, he ended up getting his own cigarettes!

I'm Allergic to Gray Hair

The most important thing I take away from being a parent is all your children aren't the same. Each one has its' own personality, ways, and methods of learning, so you got to learn to adapt. Although I was a single parent raising my children, I'm still so proud of how well they turned out to be in life. All of them are teachers and educators in their own way so I'm proud of them and the parents they've become.

Doris Kimbrough and Lawrence Kimbrough

Brothers: (L) Bobby Kimbrough, Alford Lee Sr., Michael Kimbrough, Gregory Kimbrough, Charles Kimbrough; Niece: Ianthe Kimbrough Nivens

Closing Remarks

I've lived a fulfilling life mostly of servitude to many people that truly makes me happy. I've served the church, The Housing Authority of Winston Salem (HAWS) and many other roles. I haven't made everyone happy, but I've given and done my best in raising my children with the tools that I had. I often think of Maya Angelou gracefully saying: *"Do the best you can until you know better. Then when you know better, do better. The question is not how to survive, but how to thrive with passion, compassion, humor and style."*

My **passion** for helping people and giving of my time and energy has brought me the most joy. My curiosity

I'm Allergic to Gray Hair

in some ways was good because it deepened my hunger to know more and educate myself more when I was told I couldn't. My **compassion** for people helped me to learn what was right and what was wrong and make the adjustments in my life to reflect that. People called it crazy, but I found **humor** in every opportunity I could. Learning to laugh throughout life is good for the soul. And doing so with a little **style** never hurts! I always look forward to the moments when my daughters and granddaughters come pick me up and we get a little retail shopping in! I'd like to think they got their classy style from me as I got it from my mother. If it's three things I'd like you as a reader to draw from this book, it's:

Closing Remarks

1. Love is a requirement from the Almighty in order to live a fulfilling life. I haven't always lived by this, but I had to learn. I had to forgive, and truly put it behind me. I had to find the lesson in life situations for me so I could grow. Sure, there were then and still are now some evil and cruel people who hurt us. Sometimes, you feel they don't deserve to be loved but the truth of the matter is they do. They need it the most because somewhere in their life is a disconnect to truly understanding what love is about. You still need to do your part by loving them anyway and showing it.

2. To accomplish anything in life you got to have **faith**. You must believe that you deserve to be your best and

give your all. You're given life by God, and it's up to you to make use of that gift by appreciation. You may not have all the tools needed to make the best of a situation, but you can put forth every effort to get the tools. Put yourself in a position to believe you're worthy of it and it'll come to you at the right time. But it most certainly takes effort. You got to start by having solid faith.

3. The combination of the two listed above is the key to it all. It takes you putting in **work** to succeed. You must apply what you're working on. I'm not talking about the physical work. I'm talking about true growth in life so you can be happy. You must be willing to work on yourself. Work hard to be kind to everyone not just a few. Work hard

towards not hurting others' feelings. Work hard towards getting along with others. None of these things come naturally; so that's why you must keep doing it. You can't accomplish it with one try.

If you find time to focus on these three points in your life, whatever your age is, you too will live a fulfilling life. I know everyone isn't blessed to live to see ninety-five, but I want you to know I don't take that for granted. As a mother, I've lost two sons in death; and there's not a moment that doesn't cross my mind and I wonder how I am still here? I have a large family that started from Miss Janie Brown and myself. To watch my children, grow and have families of their own, on down

I'm Allergic to Gray Hair

to giving me grandchildren and great-great grandchildren is such a beautiful thing. The times we get together and celebrate birthdays, holidays or sometimes just to have family time is what it's all about. We get out and travel to see all this big world has to offer. Showing my grandchildren and great-grandchildren pictures of their parents when they were little is so funny to see their reactions. We still sing and quite a few of us are on the choir at our churches. One of the highlights for me was last year watching my grandson being sworn in as the first black Sheriff for Forsyth County. The same county that's home to me and the same city where I experienced firsthand racism to the highest degree. I'm here to witness that and it means so much to me to be a part of that history. I guess it's safe to say by now you've figured out me being allergic to old gray headed folks was cured as I'm now one! I wouldn't trade it for the world and I'm ready for the next child who feels like we make them sick!

I'd tell them: "*Sit down, let me tell you a few stories that made me sick!*"

Co-Author's Thank You Poem

Thank you for walking with me on
my special journey of life
Many days filled with happiness,
sadness, and strife
Maybe in one chapter you found a
special or familiar story
I've appreciated your company, so
I'm saying:
"To God be the glory!"

Doris Norwilla Brown Kimbrough

References

https://blackpast.org/aah/st-philips-moravian-church-winston-salem-north-carolina-1822

https://northcarolinaroom.wordpress.com/2012/02/15/help-preserve-happy-hill-heritage/

https://triadculturalarts.org/index.php/happy-hill-shotgun-house-project/

http://www.haws.org/documents/ar_2008.pdf

I'm Allergic to Gray Hair

www.ingramcontent.com/pod-product-compliance
Lightning Source LLC
Chambersburg PA
CBHW052051070526
44584CB00017B/2125